Looking Inside

Cells

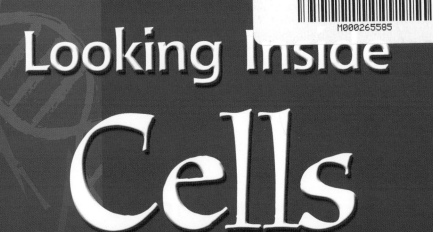

Kimberly Fekany Lee, Ph.D.

Life Science Readers:
Looking Inside Cells

Publishing Credits

Editorial Director
Dona Herweck Rice

Creative Director
Lee Aucoin

Associate Editor
Joshua BishopRoby

Illustration Manager
Timothy J. Bradley

Editor-in-Chief
Sharon Coan, M.S.Ed.

Publisher
Rachelle Cracchiolo, M.S.Ed

Science Contributor
Sally Ride Science™

Science Consultants
Thomas R. Ciccone, B.S., M.A.Ed.
Chino Hills High School
Dr. Ronald Edwards,
DePaul University

Teacher Created Materials

5301 Oceanus Drive
Huntington Beach, CA 92649-1030
http://www.tcmpub.com
ISBN 978-0-7439-0583-1

Table of Contents

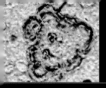

A Look at Cells

↑ Matthias Schleiden

↑ Rudolf Virchow

Have you ever seen a **cell**? Cells are the smallest unit of life. They are called the building blocks of life. We cannot see individual cells with our naked eyes. We must use a microscope to see them.

The importance of cells is outlined in the **Cell Theory**. Three scientists developed the Cell Theory in the 1800s. They were Matthias Schleiden (mah-TEE-ahs SHLAHYD-n), Rudolf Virchow (ROO-dawlf FIR-koh), and Theodor Schwann (TEY-oh-dawr shvahn). The Cell Theory has three parts. First, all living things are made of one or more cells. Second, cells are the basic unit of life of all living things. Third, all cells come from other cells.

In many ways, plant and animal cells are similar. But there are also differences. For example, plant and animal cells have different structures. You will learn about them.

Did You Know?

The average human is made of more than 75 trillion cells.

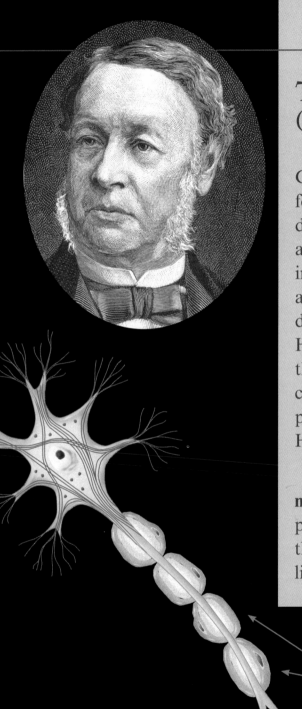

Theodor Schwann
(1810–1882)

Theodor Schwann was born in Germany. He was a physiologist. He focused his research on animals. He discovered that, like plants, all animals are made of cells. He also made other important discoveries. He discovered a protein called pepsin. It helps break down food in our digestive system. He studied nerve cells. He discovered that some of the extensions of nerve cells have a protective covering. This protective covering is made of cells. He called them **Schwann cells**.

Have you ever heard the word **metabolism**? Schwann was the first person to use this word. It describes the chemical changes that occur in living things.

Schwann cells on a nerve cell

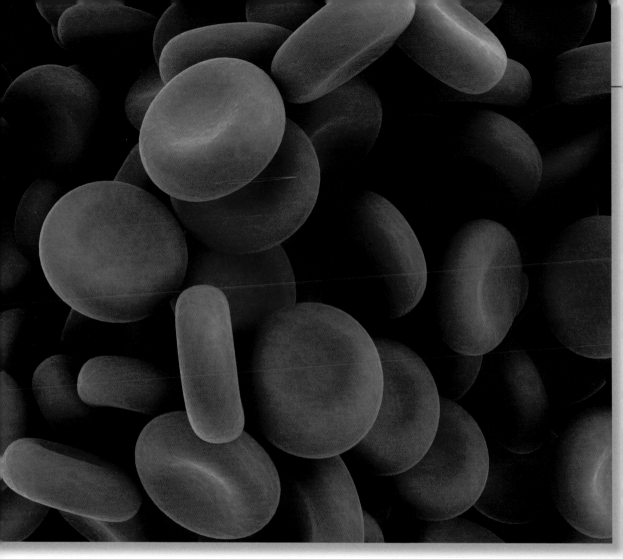

 red blood cells

Cell Shape and Size

In both plants and animals there are different types of cells. Cells with different **functions** often have different shapes that match their jobs. Animals have red blood cells. These cells must travel quickly through small tubes. So, they are shaped like balls that have been squeezed in the middle. Another type of animal cell is a nerve cell. These send signals to and from our brains. These signals must often travel long distances. Nerve cells are usually long and skinny.

You may think that large cells are better than small cells. Actually, the opposite is true. If cells get too big, then they cannot function well. A larger surface area means that there is more area for **substances** to enter and exit cells. A smaller inside area means that substances have a smaller distance to travel to get from one side of a cell to the other.

nerve cells

Cell Membranes

Plant and animal cells are surrounded by a cell **membrane.** The cell membrane is flexible. It acts like the **gatekeeper** of a cell. It controls what goes in and out of cells. Some substances move easily through the cell membrane. Other substances cannot move through it.

The cell membrane of a plant cell is surrounded by a cell wall. Cell walls are not as flexible as cell membranes. They are stronger than cell membranes. They help to support plants. When you water a plant, the plant moves water into its cells. The cell membrane pushes against the cell wall. The cell wall is rigid. It limits the size of a plant cell. Animal cells do not have cell walls. If an animal cell receives too much water, the cell will burst. It is like a balloon that is filled with too much air.

cell membrane

cell wall

Robert Brown (1773–1858)

Robert Brown was born in Scotland. He was a **botanist.** He spent years in Australia. He collected plants. He identified over 2,000 new plant species. A number of plant species have been named after him.

Brown made many notable discoveries in the field of cell biology. He studied orchids and other plants. He found that all plant cells had a round structure in the middle of the cell. He named it the nucleus. Later, scientists found that the nucleus controls a cell's activities. It holds the cell's DNA and gives instructions on what proteins the cell should make.

Robert Brown

Moving In and Out of Cells

Substances must travel in and out of cells. **Diffusion** is one way that substances can do so. It does not require any energy. Diffusion is when substances move from an area of high **concentration** to an area of low concentration.

It is like dropping food coloring into a cup of water. When you first drop it, it stays in one ball. But in time, it spreads throughout the water. All of the water gets colored. The color moves from an area of high concentration to a low one.

Diffusion is usually a slow process. Sometimes it is made easier by **proteins.** They make a channel through the cell membrane. This kind of diffusion is called facilitated diffusion.

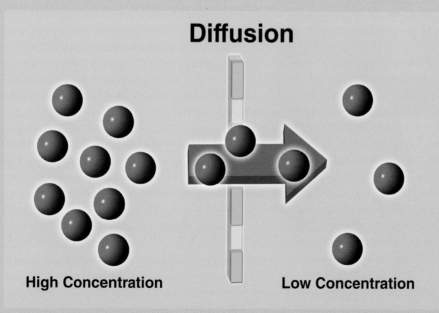

Diffusion

High Concentration   **Low Concentration**

Diffusion lets molecules move from one side of a membrane to the other until an equal number of molecules are on both sides of the membrane.

Can You Smell It?

Diffusion is not just for cells. Can you smell an odor from across the room? Substances in the air also travel by diffusion.

the diffusion of food coloring in water

Cells take in nutrients and expel waste through diffusion.

Cytoplasm and Organelles

Plant and animal cells are filled with fluid that is like gelatin. The fluid is called **cytoplasm** (SY-toh-plaz-uhm). It is made of cytosol (SY-toh-sawl). Cytosol is like a special soup that has everything the cell needs to live.

A cell must do many different jobs to survive. Inside the fluid, there are many different cells parts called organelles (or-guh-NELS). Each **organelle** does a different job. Some organelles turn food into energy. Other organelles store water. Most organelles are separated from the cytosol by a membrane. The membrane is like a skin that only lets in what the organelle needs. Everything else is kept outside.

One special kind of organelle is called **chloroplast**. Plant cells have these. Chloroplasts turn sunlight into energy that the rest of the cell can use. Animals do not have chloroplasts. They must get their energy from eating other things.

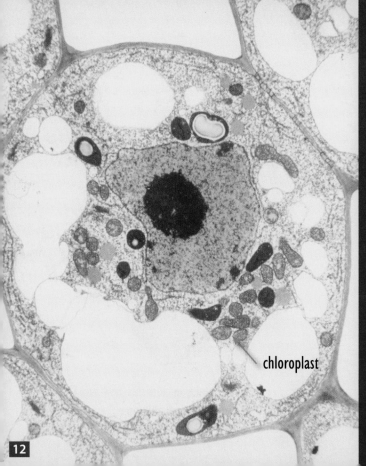

chloroplast

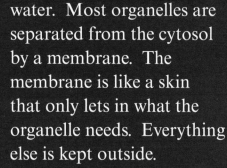

← plant cell   animal cell →

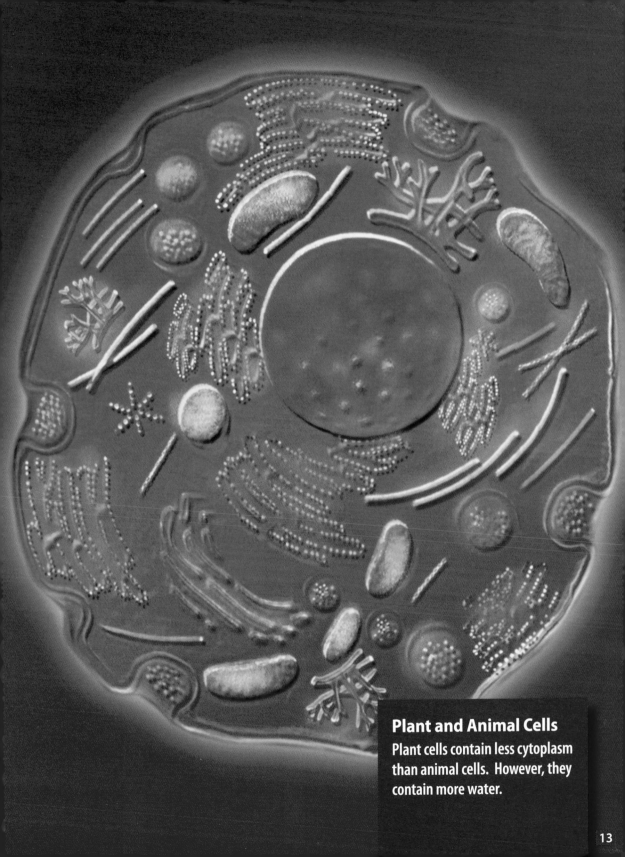

Plant and Animal Cells
Plant cells contain less cytoplasm than animal cells. However, they contain more water.

13

Controlling the Cell

The **nucleus** of a cell is often called the control center of a cell. The nucleus directs what happens in a cell. It controls the cell's growth and **reproduction.** How can the nucleus direct these activities? The nucleus contains the **chromosomes** of a cell. Chromosomes are long, threadlike structures. They are made of **DNA.** Chromosomes and DNA are what make each species unique. They make each individual unique, too.

The nucleus is surrounded by a nuclear membrane. It has pores that allow some substances to pass in and out of the nucleus. DNA never leaves the nucleus. The information carried by DNA is transferred to another molecule called RNA, or ribonucleic (ry-bow-noo-KLAY-ik) acid. RNA can exit the nucleus. The RNA gives instructions to ribosomes (RI-bow-zohms) to make different proteins. Cells' proteins affect what they are like and what they can do. It all starts with the chromosomes in DNA.

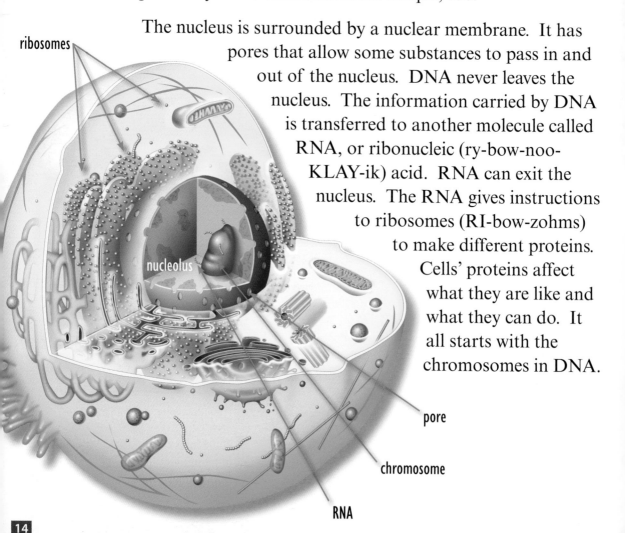

ribosomes

nucleolus

pore

chromosome

RNA

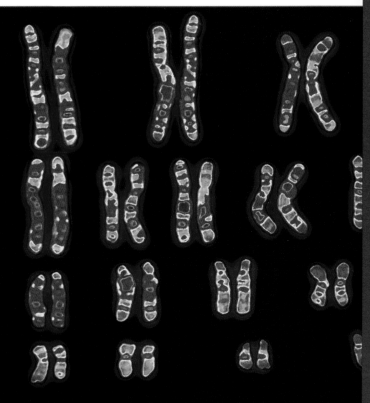

human chromosomes

Human Chromosomes
Humans have 23 pairs of chromosomes.

Unique DNA
Each person has different DNA. It can be used to help solve crimes. Police can figure out people's DNA by using their blood. But, they can also use their fingernails or hair. They can then match the DNA with a data bank to help them solve the crime.

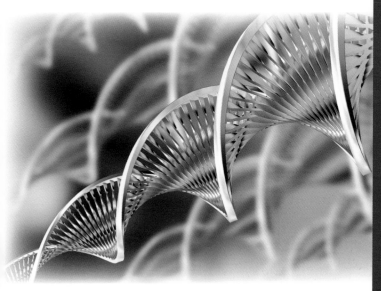

DNA curls into a shape called a double helix.

Changing Leaves

Did you ever wonder why leaves change color in the fall? It is because the chlorophyll goes out of the cells in the leaves.

Energy in Cells

Where do we get the energy we need to move, eat, and sleep? It comes from cells. **Mitochondria** (my-tuh-KON-dree-uh) are organelles that change food into energy cells can use. This is called **cellular respiration**. Cellular respiration needs oxygen. Mitochondria break apart molecules of food and release the energy. Then the cell uses the energy to build new proteins, move molecules around the cell, and make more cells.

Both plant and animal cells have mitochondria. Plant cells have chloroplasts, too. These are organelles that use energy from light. Chloroplasts contain a **pigment.** It is called **chlorophyll** (KLOR-uh-fil). Chlorophyll absorbs energy from the sun or other sources of light. The chloroplast uses that energy to make food from water and carbon dioxide. This process of making food is called **photosynthesis** (foh-tuh-SIN-thuh-sis). The green pigment is also what makes plants green.

mitochondrion

chloroplast

Skulls and Disabilities
Virchow studied the skulls of disabled persons. He wanted to determine what caused their disabilities.

Rudolf Virchow (1821–1902)

Rudolph Virchow was a German doctor. He held many other titles, too. He is known for his contribution to cell theory. He found that every cell orginates from another cell. He is considered the founder of **cellular pathology.** He believed that disease is caused by cells, not organs or tissues.

Virchow was also elected to the Berlin City Council. He actively worked toward improving sewage disposal and school hygiene. He designed two hospitals. He even established a way to do autopsies.

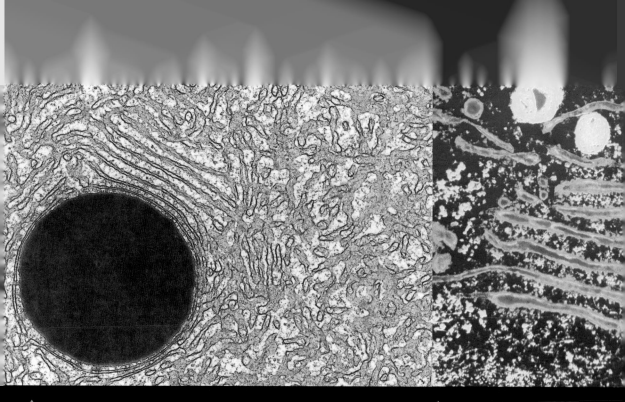

↑ smooth endoplasmic reticulum   ↑ rough endoplasmic reticulum

Cell Factories

Cells have many jobs. One of their jobs is to make new molecules. The cell might use these molecules. Or, the molecules may be sent out to be used by a different cell.

Smooth **endoplasmic reticulum** (EN-duh-plaz-mik ruh-TIK-yuh-luhm), or ER, is an organelle. Smooth ER is a series of folded membranes. Its job is to make substances called **lipids.** Lipids store energy, build cell parts, and send messages. There is also rough ER. Rough ER can make lipids as well as proteins. Proteins are building blocks for many things a cell needs to do.

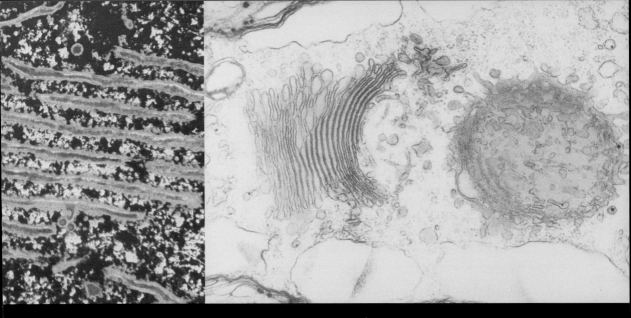

↑ Golgi body

Lipids and proteins are made in the ER. After they are made, they usually go to another organelle. This other organelle is called the **Golgi** (GAWL-jee) **body**.

The Golgi body is made of stacks of flattened membranes. It puts the lipids and proteins into membrane packages. The packages let substances travel to other parts of the cell. Some packages fuse with the cell membrane. The substances are then released to the outside of the cell.

Feeling Better?

Do you go to the doctor when you are sick? Has she ever given you an antibiotic to make you better? Some antibiotics work by attacking the ribosomes of bacteria.

Cell Storage

Do you have cabinets and closets in your home? What do you store in them? Do you store food and clothes? Cells also have storage places. They have membrane-bound storage places. They are called **vacuoles** (VAK-yoo-ohls). Vacuoles provide temporary storage for water, food, waste products, and other materials used by the cell. Animal cells usually have many cell vacuoles. Plant cells usually have a very large vacuole that stores water for the plant. The vacuole increases in size when water is plentiful. It decreases in size when there is less water available for the plant.

The vacuole of a plant cell shrinks and expands. When it is full of water and expanded, the leaves of a plant are rigid. When plants need water, the leaves droop.

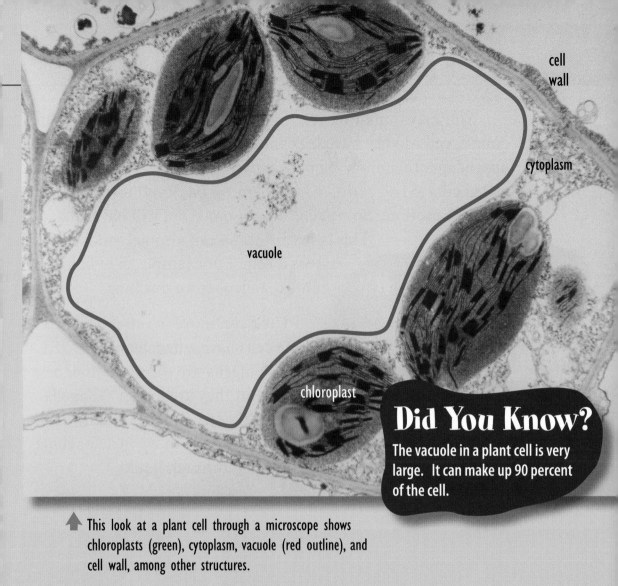

cell wall

cytoplasm

vacuole

chloroplast

Did You Know?

The vacuole in a plant cell is very large. It can make up 90 percent of the cell.

This look at a plant cell through a microscope shows chloroplasts (green), cytoplasm, vacuole (red outline), and cell wall, among other structures.

Cells do not only have vacuoles to store materials. They also have organelles to recycle and remove unwanted materials. **Lysosomes** (LY-so-zomes) are organelles. They contain chemicals that digest unwanted materials. They break down old, worn-out cell parts, cell waste, and food molecules. It is very important that lysosomes have a membrane separating the digestive chemicals from the rest of the cell. Otherwise, the digestive chemicals would break down parts of the cell that were still needed.

Cell Movement

You may think that cells cannot move. Some cells do! Of course, cells do not have legs and feet. But some cells do have **appendages** that allow them to move. Cells may have tiny hairs called **cilia** (SIL-ee-uh). The cilia move back and forth in a wavelike motion. Some cells do not move but still have cilia. This is because cilia can also help move fluid across a cell. For example, cilia help remove mucus from our lungs.

Cells can move in other ways, too. Some cells have a **flagellum** (fluh-JEL-uhm). Flagella are the same thickness as cilia. But they are longer. Flagella are long, whiplike structures. Usually cells have only one flagellum. Cells with flagella move in a snakelike motion. This allows the cell to swim through liquid.

⬇ cell with cilia

⬇ cells with flagella

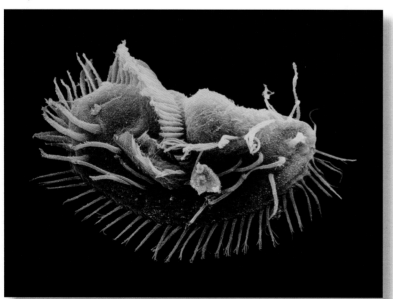

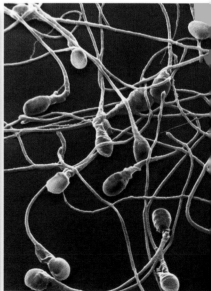

Rita Levi-Montalcini
(1909–)

Rita Levi-Montalcini was born in Italy. Her parents were very smart. Her father was also very traditional. He felt that a career would interfere with her role as a mother and wife. She begged her father. He finally allowed her to go to school. She went to medical school and graduated at the top of her class.

World War II started. Jews were not allowed to practice medicine. So, she did her research with chick **embryos** in secret. Toward the end of the war, she was hired as a medical doctor. She worked with people who had become ill during the war. After the war, she became a professor.

Then she joined a researcher in the United States. The two scientists led more experiments with chick embryos. She became a professor in the United States and started a research unit in Rome. She researched many things. Her work has helped treat many types of injuries and diseases. She may best be known for her study of chemicals that help cells grow. She even won a Nobel Prize.

Cytoskeleton

Can you imagine your body without bones? Your body would have no support. You wouldn't be able to move. Your skeleton provides support. It allows you to move. Cells also have a kind of skeleton. It's called the **cytoskeleton** (sy-tuh-SKEL-uh-tuhn). It gives support for the cell. It also adds to the cell's shape and cell movement. It is not a constant structure. The cytoskeleton can be built, taken apart, and rebuilt. The cell's shape changes every time.

microtubules (green) in a cell

The cytoskeleton is not made of bones. It is made of thin, hairlike fibers. There are three different kinds of fibers. The first is a microtubule. It is a hollow tube. The second is a microfilament. It is a solid rod. The rod is made of two twisted protein chains. The third type is an intermediate filament. It is made of several chains of proteins. The chains are coiled into a thick cable. Intermediate filaments are larger in diameter than microfilaments. Whatever the shape of the fibers, their job is to support the cell.

Cell Crawling

Some cells move when the filaments are broken down and rebuilt. This is often called cell crawling.

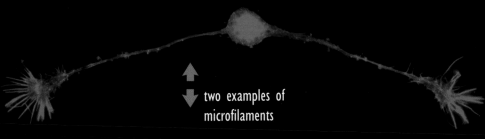

two examples of microfilaments

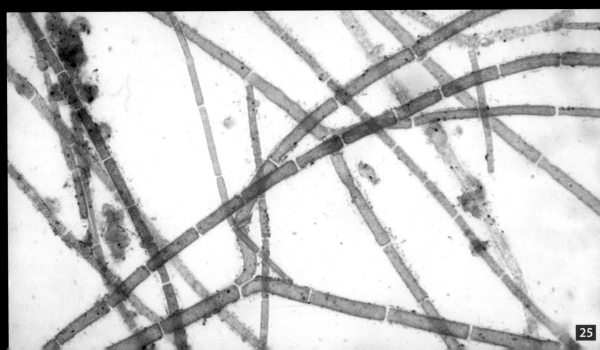

Making More Cells

Do you remember the three parts of cell theory? One part is that all cells come from other cells. New cells are made when a cell divides. Cells divide by a process called **mitosis.** Something happens before mitosis. The DNA of a cell is copied. During mitosis, the cell splits into two daughter cells. Each daughter cell gets one of the copies of the DNA. Mitosis produces two daughter cells with identical DNA. They come from one parent cell. The DNA in the daughter cells is an exact copy of the DNA in the original parent cell.

New cells must be produced for many reasons. Most animals and plants grow over time. They grow because the number of cells increases. New cells are also made to replace old cells or damaged cells. Some animal cells have to reproduce very quickly. The cells in our stomachs may only last a few days before stomach acid destroys them. The cells have to divide and make more cells faster than the stomach acid can destroy them.

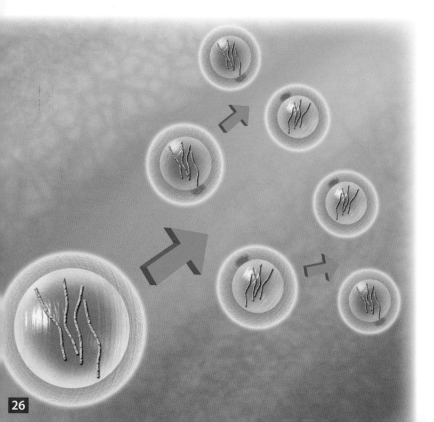

A cell with four chromosomes that divides by mitosis produces two cells. They each have the same four chromosomes. Then, those new cells can divide again.

Elaine Fuchs (1950–)

Elaine Fuchs grew up in Illinois. She has always been around science. Her father was a scientist. So was her aunt. Her sister is, too. Fuchs is a **biochemist.** She has been a university professor for over 20 years. She also does research. She studies skin biology. She studies genetic diseases such as skin cancers.

Fuchs was the first to use **reverse genetics.** This starts with knowing how a protein works. It looks at proteins that are defective, or don't work properly. Then it looks at diseases that occur with defective proteins. She also helped make dermatology (the study and care of skin) a modern-day science.

Fuchs is a professor and a researcher. She also thinks that educating children is important. She has always been excited about science. She wants children to be excited, too.

Watch It Grow!

Some bamboo plants can grow as much as 12 inches in a single day. Imagine if you grew that quickly!

Lab: Make Your Own Light Microscope

Make this simple light microscope to see how early biologists examined their specimens.

Materials

- two magnifying glasses

- a newspaper article

- a photograph

- a paper and pen to record your results

Procedure

1 Hold one magnifying glass just above the surface of the newspaper article. Then, hold it above the photo. The print and image should appear larger.

2 Move the magnifying glass higher. See how the print and photo change. They should become blurred as you move the magnifying glass higher.

3 Return the magnifying glass to the original position. Place it just above the newspaper article.

4 Get the second magnifying glass. Place it between the first magnifying glass and your eyes.

5 Move the second magnifying glass up and down. Get the print in clear focus. How does it look?

6 Describe what happens. Does the print appear larger or smaller than it does when you used a single magnifying glass?

7 Record your results.

8 Repeat, using the photograph.

Glossary

appendages—something added or attached to an entity of greater importance or size; for example, cells have cilia to help them move

biochemist—a scientist who specializes in the study of chemical substances and vital processes occurring in living organisms

botanist—a biologist specializing in the study of plants

cell—the smallest unit of living things

Cell Theory—states that all living things are made of cells, all cells come from other cells, and cells are the basic unit of all living things

cellular pathology—the interpretation of disease origins in terms of cellular alterations

cellular respiration—process used by cells to break down food molecules into small units of energy

chlorophyll—the green cells in plants where photosynthesis takes place

chloroplast—organelle in plants where photosynthesis occurs

chromosome—a structure made of a coiled DNA molecule that appears during mitosis and meiosis

cilia—small, hairlike extensions on some cells that are used for movement

concentration—the strength of a solution

cytoplasm—contents of a cell contained within the plasma membrane

cytoskeleton—network of fibers that help cells move, divide, and maintain their shape

diffusion—when substances move from an area of high concentration to an area of low concentration; does not require energy

digest—to turn food into simpler chemicals that can be absorbed by the body

DNA—deoxyribonucleic acid; stores the genetic material in a cell's nucleus

embryo—an animal that is developing either in its mother's womb or in an egg

endoplasmic reticulum—a membrane-bound organelle that makes and moves materials around in a cell

flagellum—long whiplike extension on some cells that is used for movement

function—the natural purpose (or job) of something

gatekeeper—someone or something that controls what can come in and what can go out

Golgi body—membrane-bound organelle that modifies materials

lipid—a substance such as fat that dissolves in alcohol but not in water and is an important part of living cells

lysosome—membrane-bound organelle that contains chemicals for digesting unwanted cell materials

membrane—a thin, flexible layer of tissue covering surfaces or organs of an animal or a plant

metabolism—all the chemical processes in your body, especially those that cause food to be used for energy and growth

mitochondria—membrane-bound organelle where cellular respiration occurs

mitosis—the process of cell division or asexual reproduction

nucleus—large membrane-bound organelle that controls the activities of a cell

organelle—membrane-bound structure in the cytoplasm of a cell

photosynthesis—process used by plant cells to make food molecules from light energy, water, and carbon dioxide

pigment—a substance that gives something a particular color when it is present in it or is added to it

proteins—fundamental components of all living cells that are essential in the diet of animals for the growth and repair of tissues

reproduction—production of young plants and animals through a sexual or asexual process

reverse genetics—the application of human gene mapping to clone the gene responsible for a particular disease when no information about the biochemical basis of the disease is available

Schwann cells—the cells that make up the protective covering of nerve cell extensions

substance—that which has mass and occupies space

vacuole—organelles in plant cells that contain large amounts of water and salt used to produce energy

Index

Sally Ride
Science

Sally Ride Science

Sally Ride Science™ is an innovative content company dedicated to fueling young people's interests in science. Our publications and programs provide opportunities for students and teachers to explore the captivating world of science—from astrobiology to zoology. We bring science to life and show young people that science is creative, collaborative, fascinating, and fun.

Image Credits